There are Plants in the Garden

by Daxxton and Evangeline McGee

A garden has many plants. There are vegetables, fruits, and flowers.

Lettuce grows low on the ground.

Its leaves are wet and crisp.

An ear of corn
   shoots up on a stalk.
   Corn is yellow and sweet.

The strawberries are fresh and juicy. They ripen on the plant.

Peas hang
from the vines,

safe in their
pods.

Onions grow underground. They are full of flavor.

The sunflowers beam in the garden. The seeds will drop come fall.

Eggplants grow
purple and shiny.
They bloom at night.

The pumpkin is large and orange;

nestled in green leaves.

The cucumbers crawl across the ground.

They are cool in the shade.

Radishes are red, white, and green.

They grow with ease.

The tomatoes
hang from the vine.
They are red
and tender.

The basil is next to the tomatoes. Its leaves are green.

Potatoes grow deep in the earth.

They come out dusty and dry.

Blueberries cover the bush.
They are tasty and tangy.

Carrots are orange and crunchy.
They stick out from the dirt.

The broccoli blossoms. Its stalks grow very tall.

Many peppers
dangle from the plant.
They are sweet and
spicy.

The melon swells
on the vine.

It is pink and
watery inside.

The apples swing from
the branch. Their peels
shine in the sun.

The dandelions
decorate the garden

and send their
seeds into the wind.

It is hard work to grow a garden. It needs love and care.

About the Authors

Daxxton and Evangeline McGee are a couple based in North Carolina. Daxxton holds his MS in biology from the University of North Carolina at Greensboro, from which Evangeline also holds her BA in English. Between them there is a broad collection of creative pursuits including essays, novels, poetry, photography, and original music.

The pair took up photographing birds as a pastime, and it quickly developed into a passion for the artform and a fascination with the ecology of the animals. This culminated in their first co-authored children's book, *There are Birds in the Garden*. From there, they expanded their naturalist interests and began to observe and grow different plants. This led to their second book, *There are Plants in the Garden*. The melding of science, art, and literature, through the couple's two educational backgrounds and interests, inspires the creation of books that explore beauty in both art and nature.

By the same authors:

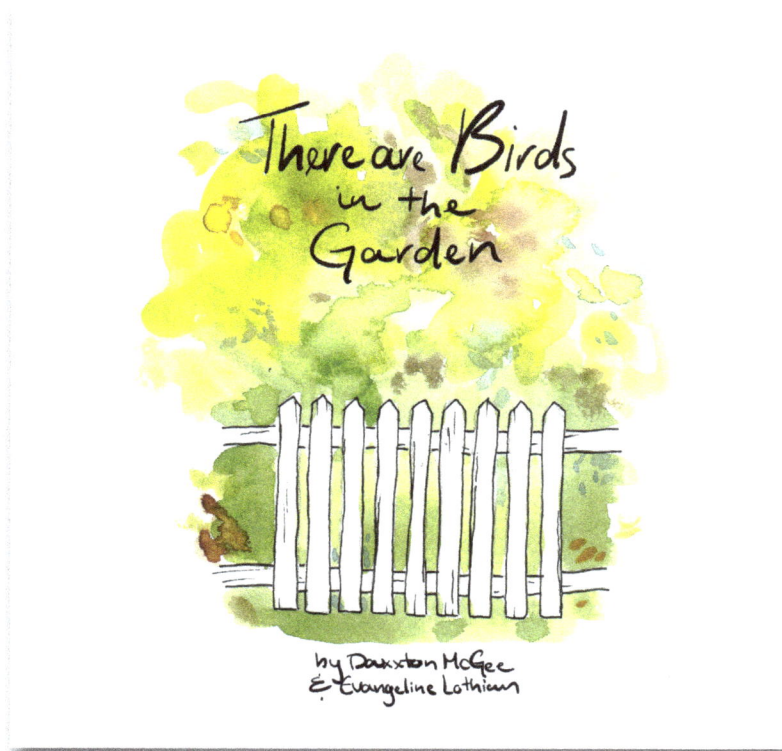

This edition published 2025
by Living Book Press

For more great books please visit www.livingbookpress.com

ISBN: 978-1-76153-918-3 (hardcover)
         978-1-922974-57-0 (softcover)

A catalogue record for this book is available from the National Library of Australia

www.ingramcontent.com/pod-product-compliance
Lightning Source LLC
Chambersburg PA
CBHW042145030426

42335CB00030B/3461